This Book Belongs to

S a o l f s

A Children's Treasury of
Lullabies

Illustrations by
Linda Bleck

STERLING CHILDREN'S BOOKS
New York

Brahms' Lullaby

Lullaby and good night,
The stars now are bright.
Creep into thy bed,
There pillow thy head.
Tomorrow thou shalt wake
When the morning doth break.
Tomorrow thou shalt wake
When the morning doth break.

Lullaby and good night,
Those blue eyes close tight.
Bright angels are near,
So sleep without fear.
They will guard thee from harm,
With fair dreamland's sweet charm.
They will guard thee from harm,
With fair dreamland's sweet charm.

Golden Slumbers

Golden slumbers kiss your eyes.
Smiles awake you when you rise.
Sleep, pretty loved ones,
Do not cry,
And I will sing a lullaby,
Lullaby, lullaby, lullaby.

Care is heavy, therefore sleep.
You are care and care must keep.
Sleep, pretty loved ones,
Do not cry,
And I will sing a lullaby,
Lullaby, lullaby, lullaby.

Sleep, Baby, Sleep

Sleep, baby, sleep,
Your papa guards the sheep.
Your mama shakes the dreamland tree,
And from it fall sweet dreams for thee.
Sleep, baby, sleep.
Sleep, baby, sleep.

Sleep, baby, sleep,
Our cottage vale is deep.
The little lamb is on the green,
With woolly fleece so soft and clean.
Sleep, baby, sleep.
Sleep, baby, sleep.

Sleep, baby, sleep,
Down where the woodbines creep.
Be always like the lamb so mild,
A kind and sweet and gentle child,
Sleep, baby, sleep.

All the Pretty Little Horses

Hush-a-bye, don't you cry,
Go to sleepy, little baby.
When you wake, you'll have cake,
And all the pretty little horses.

Black and bay, dapple and gray,
Coach and six little horses.
Hush-a-bye, don't you cry,
Go to sleepy, little baby.

Hush-a-bye, don't you cry,
Go to sleepy, little baby.
When you wake, you'll have cake,
And all the pretty little horses.

Way down yonder, down in the meadow,
There's a poor wee little lamby.
The bees and the butterflies circling where she lies,
The poor wee thing cries for her mammy.

Hush-a-bye, don't you cry,
Go to sleepy, little baby.
When you wake, you'll have cake,
And all the pretty little horses.

Rock-a-Bye, Baby

Rock-a-bye, baby,
In the treetop.
When the wind blows
The cradle will rock.
When the bough breaks
The cradle will fall,
And down will come baby,
Cradle and all.

Frère Jacques

Frère Jacques, Frère Jacques,
Dormez-vous? Dormez-vous?
Sonnez les matines,
Sonnez les matines,
Ding, Ding, Dong! Ding, Ding, Dong!

Are you sleeping? Are you sleeping?
Brother John, Brother John?
Morning bells are ringing,
Morning bells are ringing,
Ding, Ding, Dong! Ding, Ding, Dong!

All Through the Night

Sleep my child and peace attend thee,
All through the night.
Guardian angels God will send thee,
All through the night.
Soft the drowsy hours are creeping,
Hill and vale in slumber sleeping,
I my loving vigil keeping,
All through the night.

While the moon her watch is keeping,
All through the night.
While the weary world is sleeping,
All through the night.
Over thy spirit gently stealing,
Visions of delight revealing,
Breathes a pure and holy feeling,
All through the night.

Love, to thee my thoughts are turning,
All through the night.
All for thee my heart is yearning,
All through the night.
Though sad fate our lives may sever,
Parting will not last forever,
There's a hope that leaves me never,
All through the night.

Beautiful Dreamer

Beautiful dreamer, wake unto me,
Starlight and dewdrops are waiting for thee.
Sounds of the rude world, heard in the day,
Lulled by the moonlight have all passed away!

Beautiful dreamer, queen of my song,
List while I woo thee with soft melody.
Gone are the cares of life's busy throng,
Beautiful dreamer, awake unto me!
Beautiful dreamer, awake unto me!

Beautiful dreamer, out on the sea,
Mermaids are chanting the wild lorelie.
Over the streamlet vapors are borne,
Waiting to fade at the bright coming morn.

Beautiful dreamer, beam on my heart,
Even as the morn on the streamlet and sea.
Then will all clouds of sorrow depart,
Beautiful dreamer, awake unto me!
Beautiful dreamer, awake unto me!

Twinkle, Twinkle, Little Star

Twinkle, twinkle, little star,
How I wonder what you are.
Up above the world so high,
Like a diamond in the sky.
Twinkle, twinkle, little star,
How I wonder what you are!

Winkum

Winkum, Winkum, shut your eyes,
While I sing sweet lullabies,
For the dews are falling soft,
Lights are flickering up aloft,
And the moon is peeping over
Yonder hilltop, capped with clover.

Chickens long have gone to rest,
Birds lie snug within their nest,
And my darling soon will be
Sleeping like a chickadee,
For with only half a try,
Winkum, Winkum shuts her eyes.

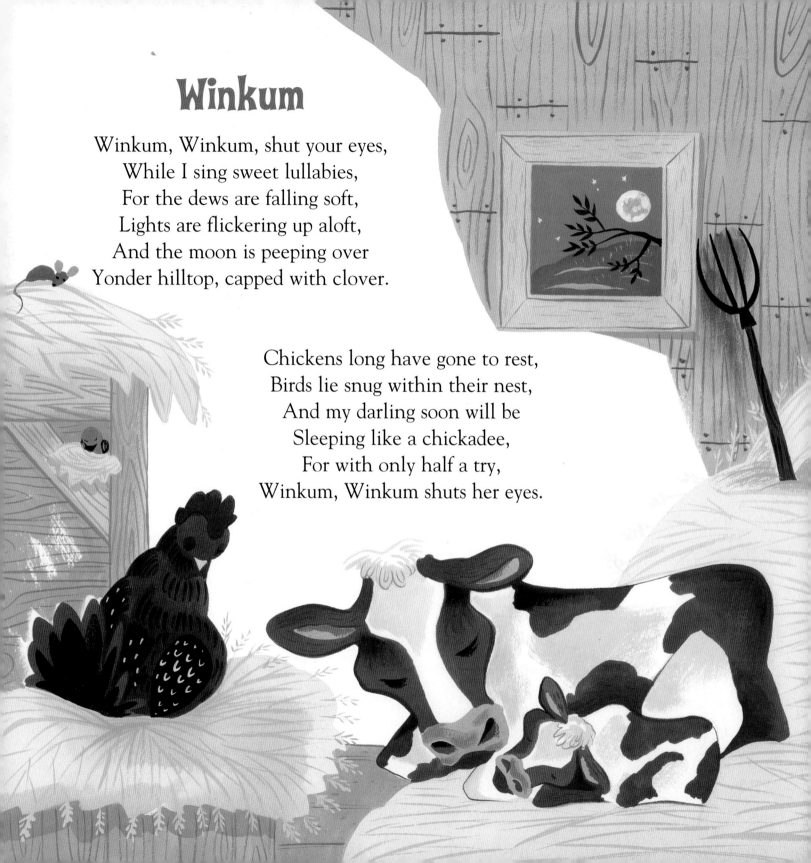

Hush Little Baby

Hush, little baby, don't say a word,
Mama's going to buy you a mockingbird.

And if that mockingbird don't sing,
Mama's going to buy you a diamond ring.

And if that diamond ring turns brass,
Mama's going to buy you a looking glass.

And if that looking glass gets broke,
Mama's going to buy you a billy goat.

And if that billy goat won't pull, Mama's going to buy you a cart and bull.

And if that cart and bull turn over,
Mama's going to buy you a dog named Rover.

And if that dog named Rover won't bark,
Mama's going to buy you a horse and cart.

And if that horse and cart fall down,
You'll still be the sweetest little baby in town.

Dance to Your Daddy

Dance to your daddy,
My little babby,
Dance to your daddy,
My little lamb!

You shall have a fishy
In a little dishy,
You shall have a fishy
When the boat comes in.

Dance to your daddy,
My little babby,
Dance to your daddy,
My little lamb!

You shall have an apple,
You shall have a plum,
You shall have a rattle-basket
When your dad comes home.

Angels Watching Over Me

All night, all day,
Angels watching over me, my Lord.
All night, all day,
Angels watching over me.

Sun is a-setting in the west,
Angels watching over me, my Lord.
Sleep my child, take your rest,
Angels watching over me.

All night, all day,
Angels watching over me, my Lord.
All night, all day,
Angels watching over me.

Sweet and Low

Sweet and low, sweet and low,
Wind of the western sea,
Low, low, breathe and blow,
Wind of the western sea!
Over the rolling waters go,
Come from the dying moon, and blow,
Blow him again to me,
While my little one,
While my pretty one,
Sleeps.

Sleep and rest, sleep and rest,
Father will come to thee soon.
Rest, rest, on mother's breast,
Father will come to thee soon.
Father will come to his babe in the nest,
Silver sails all out of the west,
Under the silver moon.
Sleep my little one,
Sleep my pretty one,
Sleep.

Star Light, Star Bright

Star light, star bright,
The first star I see tonight,
I wish I may, I wish I might,
Have the wish I wish tonight.

Day Is Done

Day is done, gone the sun,
From the hills, from the lake,
From the sky.
All is well, safely rest,
God is nigh.

For my brothers and sisters, Tom, Jim, Cathie,
Marilynn, Bob, Susie, John, and Chuck. —L.B.

STERLING CHILDREN'S BOOKS
New York

An Imprint of Sterling Publishing
387 Park Avenue South
New York, NY 10016

ISBN 978-1-4549-1358-0

Library of Congress Cataloging-in-Publication Data

A children's treasury of lullabies / illustrated by Linda Bleck.
   p. cm.
 Summary: An illustrated collection of well-known lullabies.
 ISBN-13: 978-1-4027-2979-9
 ISBN-10: 1-4027-2979-0
 1. Lullabies—Texts. 2. Children's songs—Texts. [1. Lullabies. 2. Songs.] I. Bleck, Linda, ill.

PZ8.3.C4345 2006
782.42—dc22

2005034080

Distributed in Canada by Sterling Publishing
c/o Canadian Manda Group, 165 Dufferin Street
Toronto, Ontario, Canada M6K 3H6
Distributed in the United Kingdom by GMC Distribution Services
Castle Place, 166 High Street, Lewes, East Sussex, England BN7 1XU
Distributed in Australia by Capricorn Link (Australia) Pty. Ltd.
P.O. Box 704, Windsor, NSW 2756, Australia

For information about custom editions, special sales, premium and corporate purchases, please
contact Sterling Special Sales Department at 800-805-5489 or specialsales@sterlingpub.com.

Printed in China
Lot #
2 4 6 8 10 9 7 5 3 1
05/14

www.sterlingpublishing.com/kids